CEREAL

by Gretchen Will Mayo

Reading consultant: Susan Nations, M.Ed., author/literacy coach/consultant

WEEKLY WR READER®
EARLY LEARNING LIBRARY

Please visit our web site at: www.earlyliteracy.cc
For a free color catalog describing Weekly Reader® Early Learning Library's
list of high-quality books, call 1-877-445-5824 (USA) or 1-800-387-3178 (Canada).
Weekly Reader® Early Learning Library's fax: (414) 336-0164.

Library of Congress Cataloging-in-Publication Data

Mayo, Gretchen.
    Cereal / by Gretchen Will Mayo.
      p. cm. — (Where does our food come from?)
    Summary: Describes how wheat, rice, and other types of grain are grown, harvested,
and made into breakfast cereals.
    Includes bibliographical references and index.
    ISBN 0-8368-4065-8 (lib. bdg.)
    ISBN 0-8368-4072-0 (softcover)
    1. Grain—Juvenile literature. 2. Cereal products—Juvenile literature. [1. Grain.
2. Cereal products.] I. Title.
SB189.M39 2004
664'.756—dc22   2003061004

This edition first published in 2004 by
Weekly Reader® Early Learning Library
330 West Olive Street, Suite 100
Milwaukee, WI 53212 USA

Copyright © 2004 by Weekly Reader® Early Learning Library

Editor: JoAnn Early Macken
Art direction, cover and layout design: Tammy Gruenewald
Photo research: Diane Laska-Swanke

Photo credits: Cover (main), title, pp. 4, 5, 6, 7, 8, 9, 10, 11, 12, 13, 14, 15, 16, 17, 18, 19, 20 © Gregg Andersen;
cover (background) © Diane Laska-Swanke

Printed in the United States of America

1 2 3 4 5 6 7 8 9 08 07 06 05 04

Table of Contents

Do you have a favorite cereal?

Healthy Choices

Look at all the cereal puffs, pillows, flakes, and balls! There are so many to choose from! Grocery shelves hold cereals of many shapes.

Shapes are only part of the cereal picture. The protein in cereal is good for your body. Many cereals have vitamins. Many cereals have minerals, too. Cereal brings energy to hungry bodies.

A bowl of cereal gives your body protein, vitamins and minerals.

Some farmers plant many acres of grains.

Growing Grains

Cereals are made from grains, such as wheat, rice, oats, barley, and corn. Grains grow best in rich soil. The plants need moisture and sun to produce healthy grains.

Rice grows in warm climates. It grows in paddy fields filled with water. Too much moisture can turn wheat, barley, corn, and oat grains moldy. With too much hot sun, the fields might dry. Insects such as locusts and corn worms can damage any crop.

Good weather helps to make a good crop.

These ripe grains are ready for harvesting.

A farmer watches the fields and hopes for the best. Cereal manufacturers buy wheat, rice, oats, and corn with large, full grains. They must be harvested at just the right time.

When the grains are ripe, huge combine machines roll into the fields. Combines harvest wheat, oats, barley, or corn in two steps. First the machines cut down the plants. Then they remove the grain.

A combine does two jobs.

Grains are kept in silos.

The harvested grain is stored until it is needed. It is kept in large, clean silos. Silos keep out dirt, moisture, and insects. The grains are taken from the silos to a cereal factory. There, the husk, or outer layer, is cleaned from each grain.

Making Cereal

Some grains are made into puffed cereal. They are usually left whole. Puffed wheat is made in a pressure chamber. The grain is heated quickly. The pressure is released, and the grains expand. The puffed wheat shoots out of the chamber. Machines add vitamins to the puffed grains.

Some grains are puffed into cereal.

Some puffs fall through the screen.

The puffs ride to an oven on a conveyor belt. They dry in hot air in the oven. Dried puffs pass over a screen. Those that are too small fall through. Only puffs of the right size are packaged. A bucket elevator carries them to the packaging machine.

Other machines make crispy rice cereal. They add moisture to rice kernels. Then the rice is heated. It pops like popcorn.

Moist rice kernels pop like popcorn.

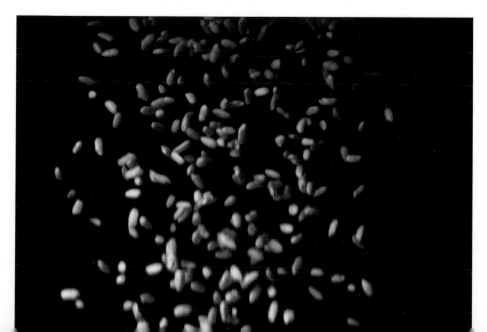

Machines help make cereal out of grains.

Some grain is turned into cereal flakes. The grain is cleaned and sorted. Then it is ground into flour.

Machines add liquid to the flour. They may also add sugar. Vitamins and minerals are added to the mix. Sheets of the mixture are baked. Baking dries the mixture. Flakes form while it is drying.

Cereal flakes are baked.

Popping in air makes the dough grow larger.

Dough can be made from oat, wheat, or corn flour. The dough can take almost any shape. A tiny dough ball can be popped in hot air. It turns into a bigger cereal ball.

Dough can also be forced through a mold. The mold gives the dough a shape. The shaped dough is cut away from the mold. Then it is puffed in hot air and dried. Alphabet, star, and animal shapes are all made this way.

Some cereals are shaped in molds.

Pour milk over granola or sprinkle
granola over ice cream.

Not all cereals are puffed, popped, or shaped.
Granola is usually made from plain oats. It is
mixed with nuts, dried fruits, seeds, and honey.
Then it is baked to make it crisp.

Plain oatmeal is one of the oldest cereals. It is still a favorite. Some oat grain is prepared just for oatmeal. Sugar, nuts, or dried fruits can be added. Wheat, rice, and bran meal make good hot cereals, too.

Hot cereal is a treat on a cold morning.

Cereal is a good choice for a snack.

Daily Grains

Cereal is not just for breakfast. Popped, exploded, or plain, cereal makes a good snack. Granola is a yummy topping for yogurt, fruit, or ice cream.

We should each eat six servings of grain foods every day. Cereal helps us grow healthy and strong.

Cereal is part of the largest group on the food pyramid.

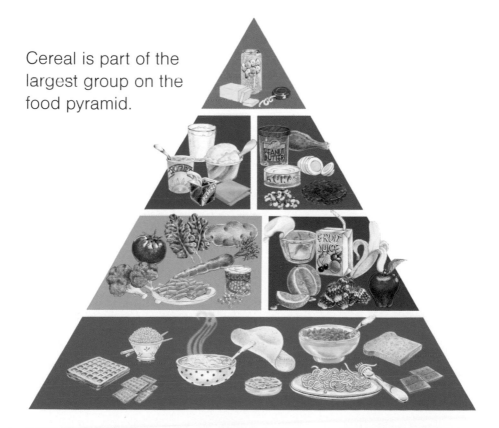

Glossary

combine — a farming machine that does more than one job

conveyor belt — a moving belt that carries products from one place to another

granola — a baked mixture of rolled oats and other ingredients

locust — a grasshopper that travels in large swarms

minerals — substances that are mined for human use and also found in human bodies

mold — a hollow container used to shape a soft substance

paddy — a flooded or irrigated area where rice is grown

pressure chamber — a closed space where air is forced against objects

protein — a substance found in all living plants and animals that is necessary for life.

For More Information

Books

Feldman, Heather. *My Breakfast: A Book About a Great Morning Meal.* *My World* Series. NY: Power Kids Press, 2000.

Julius, Jennifer. *I Like Cereal.* *Good Food* Series. NY: Children's Press, 2001.

Klingel, Cynthia and Noyed, Robert B. *Bread and Cereal.* *Let's Read About Food* Series. Milwaukee: Weekly Reader Early Learning Library, 2002.

Nelson, Robin. *Grains.* Minneapolis: Lerner, 2003.

Web Sites

Kid's World Nutrition Coloring Book
www.agr.state.nc.us/cyber/kidswrld/java/ColorBig3.htm
Paint a picture of each food group

Meals Matter: BreakFAST & Jump to it!
www.mealsmatter.org/Activities/breakfast.htm
Choose a healthy breakfast

Rice Romp
www.riceromp.com/home.cfm
Select your grade level for games and facts about rice, rice cereal, and rice flour

Index

About the Author

Gretchen Will Mayo likes to be creative with her favorite foods. In her kitchen, broccoli and corn are mixed with oranges to make a salad. She sprinkles granola on applesauce. She blends yogurt with orange juice and bananas. She experiments with different pasta sauces. When she isn't eating, Ms. Mayo writes stories and books for young people like you. She is also a teacher and illustrator. She lives in Wisconsin with her husband, Tom, who makes delicious soups. They have three adult daughters.